FOR DARCIE, MY FIRST
AND FOREVER PUPPY

Copyright © 2017 by Erika Riggs.

Published by Familius LLC, www.familius.com

Familius books are available at special discounts for bulk purchases for sales promotions or for family or
corporate use. For more information, contact Premium Sales at 559-876-2170 or email orders@familius.com.

Library of Congress Cataloging-in-Publication Data
2016962610
ISBN 9781944822866

Edited by Julia Levitan
Jacket and book design by David Miles
Special thanks to our Twitter guest photographers: @darciedog (page 9), @abbey_and_zeus (page 25),
@busybodybiscuit (page 27), @brucethefrenchbully (page 31), @missmiau (page 50),
@mars.oli (page 54), @shandandherdogs (page 59), @jasperthecowdog (page 62),
@meet_lincoln (page 104), @captain_shark (page 114), @love.a.bull_diesel (page 118),
@mylittle.cricket (page 126), @korra_the_chibi_shibe (page 130).
All photographs copyright © 2017 by their respective owners.
All other photographs and vector elements licensed from Shutterstock.com.

10 9 8 7 6 5 4 3 2 1

First Edition

Printed in China

ERIKA
RIGGS

IF IT SITS, I LICKS

THE ULTIMATE DOG QUOTEBOOK

FAMILIUS

CONTENTS

INTRODUCTION

Did you ever want something so badly as a child that you begged your parents for it, wrote Santa for it, and wished for it every year as you blew out your birthday candles. That was me. And the something I wanted so badly was a dog.

Growing up as the middle child (the third of five), there was no short-age of noise, mess, and trouble to get into (at least according to my parents). But for me, a part of our family always seemed to be missing. Sure, we had fish and the occasional mouse or hamster as pets, but it wasn't the same. I wanted a pet I could interact with. With a dog, you can play at the park, dress up, and share popcorn as you watch TV together. A dog is more than just a pet. It's a part of the family.

It wasn't until I was twenty-five that my dream of becoming a dog-mom came true. After short-listing *Petfinder* and visiting a number of animal shelters, I came across a kennel at Dallas Animal Services labeled "Husky

Mix." Inside was a tan-and-white puppy leaning against the glass door. When we walked by the kennel, "Husky Mix" looked up with her one brown eye-one blue eye, wagged her dipstick tail, and I was smitten on the spot.

We renamed her Darcie, and she is everything I begged and wished for. We play at the park, I dress her up every Halloween, and we binge watch *Friends* reruns with a bowl of popcorn between us. She's more than just a pet. She's a comforter, snuggle buddy, exercise enthusiast, pro-tector, comedian, foot warmer, and so much more. She has filled a void in my life and become the family member I've waited so long to love.

"THERE IS NOTHING TRUER IN THIS WORLD THAN THE LOVE OF A GOOD DOG."

—MIRA GRANT

CHAPTER 1

PUPPY LOVE

There's a reason that young love and infatuation have been characterized as "puppy love." Snuggle or play with one, and you'll understand that there's nothing that gives you a rush of instant adoration like a warm and wriggling puppy. Between their tiny tongues and their too-big-for-their-bodies paws, the clumsy way they run, and the way they always seem to be smiling, puppies are the embodiment of happiness.

HAPPINESS IS A WARM PUPPY.

—Charles M. Schulz

I'M CONVINCED THAT PETTING A PUPPY IS GOOD LUCK.

—MEG DONOHUE

A PUPPY IS BUT
A DOG, PLUS HIGH
SPIRITS AND MINUS
COMMON SENSE.

—Agnes Repplier

THERE IS NO PSYCHIATRIST IN THE WORLD LIKE A PUPPY LICKING YOUR FACE.

—Ben Williams

WHOEVER SAID YOU CAN'T BUY HAPPINESS FORGOT

little

PUPPIES.

—Gene Hill

NO SYMPHONY ORCHESTRA EVER PLAYED MUSIC LIKE A TWO-YEAR-OLD GIRL LAUGHING WITH A PUPPY.

—Ben Williams

CHAPTER 2

FUR BABiES

When you first get a dog, you might be under the impression that you're bringing home a pet. You might think that your new dog will learn to adapt to your personality, rambunctious kids, and rules of the house.

Give it a little time, and you'll soon realize that the dog you brought home is not a pet; it's family. Your little (or big) bundle of joy will teach you to adapt *your* lifestyle to *their* personality. They'll be the one riling up your rambunctious kids, actually helping them dig up earthworms in the backyard. And as for rules? Well, I have yet to meet someone who can say no to puppy-dog eyes.

GETTING A DOG IS LIKE
GETTING MARRIED. IT
TEACHES YOU TO BE LESS
SELF-CENTERED, TO ACCEPT
SUDDEN, SURPRISING
OUTBURSTS OF AFFECTION,
AND NOT TO BE UPSET BY A
FEW SCRATCHES ON YOUR CAR.

—BEN WILLIAMS

CHILDREN AND DOGS
ARE AS NECESSARY
TO THE WELFARE OF
THE COUNTRY AS
WALL STREET AND
THE RAILROADS.

—Harry S. Truman

WHEN YOUR CHILDREN
ARE TEENAGERS, IT'S
IMPORTANT TO HAVE A
DOG SO THAT SOMEONE
IN THE HOUSE IS
HAPPY TO SEE YOU.

—Meg Donohue

MY FASHION PHILOSOPHY IS, IF YOU'RE NOT COVERED IN DOG HAIR, YOUR LIFE IS EMPTY.

—ELAYNE BOOSLER

A DOG IS LIKE
A PERSON—HE
NEEDS A JOB
AND A FAMILY
TO BE WHAT HE'S
MEANT TO BE.

—ANDREW VACHSS

IF YOU WANT
THE BEST SEAT IN
THE HOUSE . . .
MOVE THE DOG.

—UNKNOWN

CHAPTER 3

Big 'N' SMALL

Everyone loves a puppy, but when they grow up into dogs, that's when people start to pick favorites. Do you like dogs that are big enough to ride or small enough to fit in your bag? Dogs that are short-haired or shaggy? Dogs that are purebred and pedigreed or mutts and mixes?

Dogs come in all shapes, sizes, colors, and breeds, but despite physical appearances, every dog has the same ability to love and be loved unconditionally.

MY LITTLE OLD DOG: A HEARTBEAT AT MY FEET.

—Edith Wharton

WHEN AN EIGHTY-
FIVE POUND MAMMAL
LICKS YOUR TEARS
AWAY, THEN TRIES TO
SIT ON YOUR LAP, IT'S
HARD TO FEEL SAD.

—Kristan Higgins

EVEN THE TINIEST POODLE IS LIONHEARTED, READY TO DO ANYTHING TO DEFEND HOME, MASTER, AND MISTRESS.

—Louis Sabin

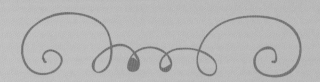

WHAT COUNTS iS NOT
NECESSARiLY THE SiZE
OF THE DOG IN THE
FiGHT—iT'S THE SIZE OF
THE FiGHT IN THE DOG.

—Dwight D. Eisenhower

EVERYONE THINKS THEY HAVE THE BEST DOG. AND NONE OF THEM ARE WRONG.

—W. R. Purche

CHAPTER 4

HUMAN'S BEST FRIEND

What are the qualities that you look for in a friend? How about someone who is dependable, honest, a good listener, and able to cheer you up after a long day? Or perhaps someone who loves you despite your flaws, who is always ready for a spontaneous beach trip, and who is more than happy to sit on the couch with you for a fourteen-hour Netflix marathon?

Chances are your dog fits all of these qualities. For dogs, our happiness is their happiness, and that's the truest form of friendship.

WHEN MOST OF US TALK TO OUR DOGS, WE TEND TO FORGET THEY'RE NOT PEOPLE.

–Julia Glass

THORNS MAY HURT
YOU, MEN DESERT YOU,
SUNLIGHT TURN TO FOG;

BUT YOU'RE NEVER
FRIENDLESS EVER,
IF YOU HAVE A DOG.

—Douglas Malloch

DOGS ARE NOT OUR WHOLE LIFE, BUT THEY MAKE OUR LIVES WHOLE.

—Roger Caras

BE THE PERSON YOUR DOG THINKS YOU ARE.

—J. W. Stephens

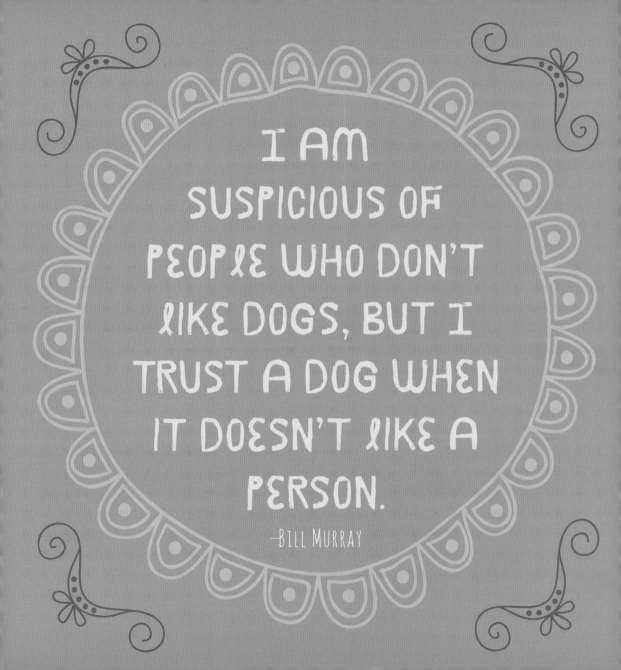

I AM SUSPICIOUS OF PEOPLE WHO DON'T LIKE DOGS, BUT I TRUST A DOG WHEN IT DOESN'T LIKE A PERSON.

—BILL MURRAY

IF A DOG WILL NOT
COME TO YOU AFTER
HAVING LOOKED YOU IN
THE FACE, YOU SHOULD
GO HOME AND EXAMINE
YOUR CONSCIENCE.

—WOODROW WILSON

CHAPTER 5

DOGS VS. CATS

There are two types of people in the world: dog people and cat people. In my own experience, these two categories can determine human compatibility faster than sports team preferences, age, or even native language. If two dog people meet, they have an instant connection based on—if nothing else—their love of dogs and their loathing of cats.

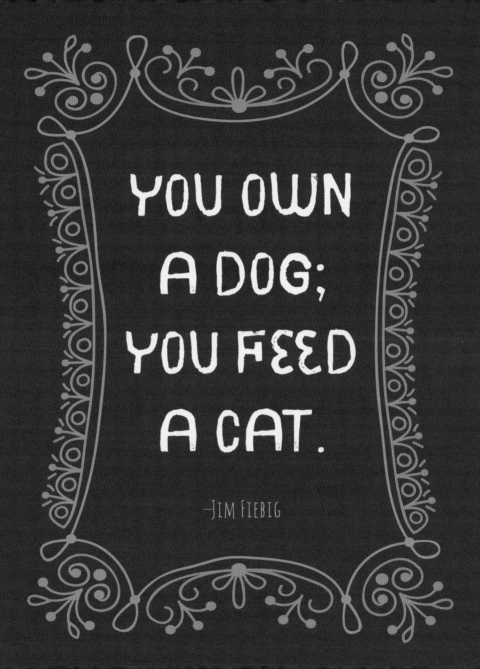

YOU OWN A DOG; YOU FEED A CAT.

—Jim Fiebig

MY TRAGEDY IS
THAT ALL i WANT
iS A DOG, AND
YET I HAVE BEEN
CURSED WITH CATS
ALL MY LiFE.

—Michael Sheen

MY CATS INSPIRE ME DAILY. THEY INSPIRE ME TO GET A DOG!

—Jim Fiebig

IN ORDER TO KEEP A TRUE
PERSPECTIVE OF ONE'S
IMPORTANCE, EVERYONE
SHOULD HAVE A DOG THAT
WILL WORSHIP HIM AND A
CAT THAT WILL IGNORE HIM.

—DEREKE BRUCE

CAT'S MOTTO: NO MATTER WHAT YOU'VE DONE WRONG, ALWAYS TRY TO MAKE IT LOOK LIKE THE DOG DID IT.

—UNKNOWN

DOGS WILL GIVE YOU
UNCONDITIONAL LOVE
UNTIL THE DAY THEY DIE.
CATS WILL MAKE YOU PAY
FOR EVERY MISTAKE YOU'VE
EVER MADE SINCE THE DAY
YOU WERE BORN.

—Oliver Gaspirtz

CHAPTER 6

WHO'S TRAINING WHO?

As dog owners, we like to think that we're in charge—that we are the masters and that we call the shots. We teach our dogs practical tricks like "sit," "lie down," and "roll over." We pay for our dogs to attend and graduate from obedience class. We reward good behavior with a treat and punish bad behavior with a tap on the nose.

Yes, we really like to think that we're in charge.

In reality, this is just an illusion. After all, who's the one carrying the poop bags during your daily walk?

A DOG TEACHES
A BOY FIDELITY,
PERSEVERANCE,
AND TO TURN
AROUND THREE
TIMES BEFORE
LYING DOWN.

—Robert Benchley

A DOOR
IS WHAT A DOG
IS PERPETUALLY
ON THE WRONG
SIDE OF.

—Ogden Nash

SCRATCH A DOG AND YOU'LL FIND A PERMANENT JOB.

—Franklin P. Jones

WE NEVER REALLY OWN A DOG AS MUCH AS HE OWNS US.

—Gene Hill

IF YOU THINK DOGS
CAN'T COUNT, TRY
PUTTING THREE DOG
BISCUITS IN YOUR
POCKET AND THEN GIVE
HIM ONLY TWO OF THEM.

—PHIL PASTORET

I FEEL SORRY FOR
PEOPLE WHO DON'T
HAVE DOGS. I HEAR
THEY HAVE TO PICK UP
FOOD THEY DROP ON
THE FLOOR.

—BILL MURRAY

CHAPTER 7

BAD DOG

Every dog goes through the "terrible twos," and some never grow out of it. But despite the chewed-up carpets and shoes, the pee puddles in the kitchen, and the inexplicable barking at two o'clock in the morning, it would never even cross your mind to live life without your dog.

Sure, you might complain to yourself as you're replanting the backyard flowers—again—but as soon as someone else mentions the holes in your flowerbed, you jump to your dog's defense.

There's really no such thing as a "bad dog."

DOGS ARE GREAT.

BAD DOGS, IF YOU CAN
REALLY CALL THEM
THAT, ARE PERHAPS
THE GREATEST OF
THEM ALL.

—JOHN GROGAN

THE MOST AFFECTIONATE CREATURE IN THE WORLD IS A WET DOG.

—Ambrose Bierce

IF YOU DON'T
WANT YOUR
DOG TO HAVE
BAD BREATH,
DO WHAT I DO:
POUR A LITTLE
LAVORIS IN
THE TOILET.

—Jay Leno

DOGS FEEL VERY STRONGLY THAT THEY SHOULD ALWAYS GO WITH YOU IN THE CAR, IN CASE THE NEED SHOULD ARISE FOR THEM TO BARK VIOLENTLY AT NOTHING RIGHT IN YOUR EAR.

—Dave Barry

A WATCHDOG

IS A DOG KEPT TO GUARD
YOUR HOME, USUALLY
BY SLEEPING WHERE
A BURGLAR WOULD
AWAKEN THE HOUSEHOLD
BY FALLING OVER HIM.

—ANONYMOUS

The thing I like most about dogs is their absolute belief in their own innocence, even when they've been caught red-handed. No matter what they've been doing, every bad dog bears the same look when scolded: "What?"

—Craig Wilson

CHAPTER 8

SIMPLE JOYS

Wouldn't it be nice if we could all live our lives the way a dog does? They have the ability to see the world as a place filled with love, adventure, and endless amounts of fun. Every day is a blessing to them, and they express their appreciation with the happy wag of their tails.

If only we could be as grateful, openly honest, loving, and able live in the moment as our dogs. Our lives and the lives of those around us would benefit, just as we benefit from our dogs.

DOGS ARE OFTEN HAPPIER THAN MEN SIMPLY BECAUSE THE SIMPLEST THINGS ARE THE GREATEST THINGS FOR THEM!

—Mehmet Murat Ildan

A DOG CAN EXPRESS MORE WITH HIS TAIL IN MINUTES THAN AN OWNER CAN EXPRESS WITH HIS TONGUE IN HOURS.

—Karen Davison

I THINK DOGS ARE THE MOST AMAZING CREATURES; THEY GIVE UNCONDITIONAL LOVE. FOR ME THEY ARE THE ROLE MODEL FOR BEING ALIVE.

—Gilda Radner

PETTING, SCRATCHING,
AND CUDDLING A DOG
COULD BE AS SOOTHING
TO THE MIND AND HEART
AS DEEP MEDITATION AND
ALMOST AS GOOD FOR
THE SOUL AS PRAYER.

—Dean Koontz

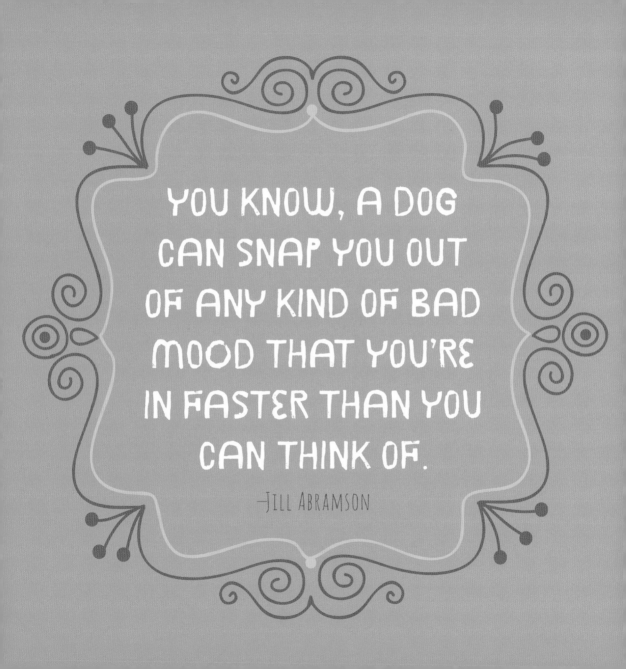

YOU KNOW, A DOG
CAN SNAP YOU OUT
OF ANY KIND OF BAD
MOOD THAT YOU'RE
IN FASTER THAN YOU
CAN THINK OF.

—JILL ABRAMSON

A DOG DESIRES
AFFECTION MORE
THAN HIS DINNER.
WELL—ALMOST!

—Charlotte Gray

THE DOG
lIVES FOR
THE DAY,
THE HOUR,
EVEN THE
MOMENT.

—Robert Falcon Scott

CHAPTER 9

ALL DOGS GO TO HEAVEN

They say that one human year is the equivalent of seven dog years, so our time with these four-legged blessings will always feel too short. Never take for granted a single day you have with your dog, and when the time comes for you to say goodbye, you'll have memories to help fill the void until you meet again.

Yes, you will meet again. After all, all dogs go to heaven.

@MYLITTLE.CRICKET

ONCE YOU
HAVE HAD A
WONDERFUL
DOG, A LIFE
WITHOUT
ONE IS A LIFE
DIMINISHED.

—DEAN KOONTZ

ONE OF THE HAPPIEST
SIGHTS IN THE WORLD
COMES WHEN A LOST
DOG IS REUNITED WITH A
MASTER HE LOVES. YOU
JUST HAVEN'T SEEN JOY
TILL YOU HAVE SEEN THAT.

—ELDON ROARK

@KORRA_THE_CHIBI_SHIBE

BEFORE YOU GET A
DOG, YOU CAN'T QUITE
IMAGINE WHAT LIVING
WITH ONE MIGHT BE LIKE;
AFTERWARD, YOU CAN'T
IMAGINE LIVING ANY
OTHER WAY.

—Caroline Knapp

IF THERE ARE NO
DOGS IN HEAVEN,
THEN WHEN I DIE, i
WANT TO GO WHERE
THEY WENT.

—WILL ROGERS

I GUESS YOU DON'T REALLY OWN A DOG; YOU RENT THEM, AND YOU HAVE TO BE THANKFUL THAT YOU HAD A LONG LEASE.

—JOE GARAGIOLA

THE BOND WITH A DOG IS AS LASTING AS THE TIES OF THIS EARTH WILL EVER BE.

—Konrad Lorenz

CHAPTER 10

LOVE AND LOYALTY

The number of occupations available to a dog is proof of both their high intelligence and their desire to protect and please humankind. We trust Police K9 Units with our safety, search-and-rescue dogs with our lives, and therapy dogs with our happiness.

But the most important job a dog can do is to be a part of our family, because that is when we trust them with our love. As with their other jobs, they are overqualified for the position. When you love a dog, you never have to worry about rejection, disappointment, or abandonment because they will *always* love you in return.

DID YOU KNOW
THAT THERE
ARE OVER THREE
HUNDRED WORDS
FOR "love" IN
CANINE?

—Gabrielle Zevin

DOGS JUST NEED YOU AND LOVE— THAT'S ALL.

—Jennifer Westfeldt

IF THE KINDEST
SOULS WERE
REWARDED WITH
THE LONGEST
LIVES, DOGS WOULD
OUTLIVE US ALL.

—UNKNOWN

TO ERR IS HUMAN—
TO FORGIVE, CANINE.

—UNKNOWN

IF I COULD BE
HALF THE PERSON
MY DOG IS, I'D
BE TWICE THE
HUMAN I AM.

—CHARLES YU

ABOUT THE AUTHOR

Erika Riggs graduated from Brigham Young University with a BA in Communications (Advertising emphasis) and an English minor. She is the middle of five children and was raised on the stage singing, dancing, and acting. Combining her love for imagination, expression, and words, she found the perfect job at Familius working as Marketing Director for the publishing house.

ABOUT FAMILIUS

Welcome to a place where parents are celebrated, not compared. Where heart is at the center of our families, and family is at the center of our homes. Where boo-boos are still kissed, cake beaters are still licked, and mistakes are still okay. Welcome to a place where books—and family—are beautiful. Familius: a book publisher dedicated to helping families be happy.

Website: www.familius.com
Facebook: www.facebook.com/paterfamilius
Twitter: @familiustalk, @paterfamilius1
Pinterest: www.pinterest.com/familius
Instagram: @familiustalk